FLY, BUTTERFLY

by Bonnie Bader

Grosset & Dunlap
An Imprint of Penguin Group (USA) LLC

The wind blows softly, tickling the leaves of a milkweed plant.

The air is sticky and sweet.

It is summer.

A butterfly flutters her wings.

She is searching for something—a leaf, still moist from the recent rain, hidden at the bottom of the milkweed plant.

FLY, BUTTERFLY

GROSSET & DUNLAP
Published by the Penguin Group
Penguin Group (USA) LLC, 375 Hudson Street, New York, New York 10014, USA

USA | Canada | UK | Ireland | Australia | New Zealand | India | South Africa | China

penguin.com
A Penguin Random House Company

Photo credits: cover: © Thinkstock; page 1: © Thinkstock; page 3: © Thinkstock; page 4: © Getty/Thorpe Griner; page 5: © Thinkstock; page 6: © Alice Cahill/Getty; page 7: © Ingo Arndt/naturepl.com; page 8: © Visuals Unlimited/naturepl.com; page 9: © Thinkstock; page 10: © Thinkstock; page 11: © Thinkstock; page 12: © Thinkstock; page 13: © Thinkstock; page 14: © Altrendo Nature/Getty; page 15: © Thinkstock; page 16: © Thinkstock; page 17: © Medford Taylor/Getty; page 18–19: © Thinkstock; page 20: © Medford Taylor/Getty; page 21: © Thinkstock; page 22: © Ken Stilger/Getty; page 23: © Deborah Harrison/Getty; page 24–25: © Thinkstock; page 26: © Thinkstock; page 27: © Nature Picture Library; page 28 : © Erik Von Weber/Getty; page 29: © Thinkstock; page 30: © Paulo Cruz/Getty; page 31: © Anthony Mercieca/Getty; page 32: © Kerri Wile/Getty.

Text copyright © 2014 by Bonnie Bader. Published by Grosset and Dunlap, a division of Penguin Young Readers Group, 345 Hudson Street, New York, New York 10014. GROSSET & DUNLAP is a trademark of Penguin Group (USA) LLC. Manufactured in China.

Library of Congress Cataloging-in-Publication Data is available.

ISBN 978-0-448-47919-4 (pbk)   10 9 8 7 6 5 4 3 2 1
ISBN 978-0-448-47920-0 (hc)   10 9 8 7 6 5 4 3 2 1

Silently, she lands.
This is the perfect place.

The perfect place to leave something special—the perfect place to lay an egg.

Now the butterfly has flown away.
She has left her egg behind.
The wind blows, scattering many green leaves.
But the egg stays on the leaf of the milkweed plant.

The egg is round—not a perfect circle, but round enough—with a hard shell to protect it.

And there is a hole in the egg.

A tiny hole, but just the same, a hole to let in air and water and sun.

So the larva inside the egg can grow.

And grow and grow and grow.

Now the larva has three pairs of legs.
And a jaw that is very strong.
It is hungry.
It eats its way out of the egg.
The larva, which is now called
a caterpillar, is free.
The sun hangs low in the sky.
It is still summer.

The caterpillar is hungry.

It eats and eats and eats the leaves of the milkweed plant.

The caterpillar gets bigger and sheds its skin.

It eats some more and gets even bigger and sheds its skin again and again and again.

Now the caterpillar has had enough to eat.
So it looks for a place where it will be safe from birds and insects and the garden cat.
Slowly, slowly, the caterpillar crawls onto another branch of the milkweed plant.

The caterpillar makes a pad of silk, and hooks itself onto the pad.

It hangs upside down from the branch, looking very much like the letter *J*.

The wind blows, scattering leaves—orange, red,
and gold—and bits of brown grass.

It is now fall.

The caterpillar sheds its skin one last time.

The sun shines, its rays bouncing off the
caterpillar's jade-green skin.

The caterpillar, now called a chrysalis, hangs
upside down from the branch.

The chrysalis hangs on tightly to the branch.

And it is still.

But only on the outside.

Inside the chrysalis, something is changing.

A great, big, miraculous change.

Gone is the caterpillar's body.

Now there are wings—orange and yellow and black.

It is time!
The chrysalis cracks open.
A butterfly emerges.
But she is small and weak, and she cannot fly yet.
Her wings are tiny and crumpled and wet.

She clings to the chrysalis as blood pumps through her body.
The butterfly must wait until she is strong enough to fly.

The butterfly's wings get bigger.
Her body dries off.
The wind blows softly, tickling
the branch.

The butterfly takes off and lands
on top of a purple flower.

Using her straw-like tongue,
she takes a long, sweet drink of the
flower's nectar.

The air smells spicy and is damp.
It is still fall.
Soon it will be too cold for the butterfly,
with her delicate wings of orange and gold.

So she flies.
Not alone, but with other butterflies.
Hundreds of butterflies.
For thousands of miles.
Clouds of butterflies
glide on wisps of wind.

When the butterflies are tired, they stop to rest, turning trees orange and yellow and black.

When they are thirsty, they stop to drink.
Lakes shimmer with the butterflies' reflections.

Then they
fly some more—
over green forests
and silver cities.

They stop to sip nectar from flowers.

And they feel strong—strong
enough to fly over the mountains of
the Sierra Madre Oriental.

At last, the butterfly can rest.
She has made the journey to Mexico.
It is winter.
But it is a kinder winter here.
No harsh winds.
No sleet or snow.

The butterfly looks for a place—a safe place to rest and spend the winter.
The butterfly sleeps a fir tree.
Safe.
But she is not alone.
She is with other butterflies.
They are all nestled in the branches and on the bark of the fir trees.

The butterfly sleeps.

Sometimes she stirs or wakes up a bit.
But mostly she rests, waiting for the winter to end.

Now it is spring!
It is time to wake up.
Time for the butterfly to fly home.
She will begin her journey with other butterflies.
But she will not fly all the way home.

The butterfly flies north.

She is searching for something—a leaf, still moist from the recent rain, hidden at the bottom of the milkweed plant.

Silently, she lands.

This is the perfect place.
The perfect place to leave something
special—the perfect place to lay an egg.
Now the butterfly is gone.
But she has left behind an egg.

And a new butterfly's life will begin.